LEANING IN

Antrim House

LEANING IN

For Joan —

Poems by

Norah Pollard

Best Wishes,

Norah Pollard

Antrim House
Hoskins Crossing, CT

Printed in the United States of America

Library of Congress Control Number: 2003102226

ISBN 0-9662783-6-4

First Edition

2003

Cover: *Connecticut River, Late Spring* (detail) by Eugene Conlon
reproduced with the kind permission of Marie Conlon

Photograph of author: Lynn Muniz

Pollard family photograph courtesy of *The Providence Journal*

ACKNOWLEDGMENTS

My deep thanks go out to my loved friends who have believed in me and supported me all along the way, and in all the ways they knew—especially Cathy Seigel, Judy Hyde, Rennie McQuilkin, Lynn Muniz, Jana Harris, Barbara and Grekim Jennings, Bob Shaw, Marilyn Barr, and Tom McDade. I would also like to thank my teachers, Dick Allen and Stephen Dunn, for their counsel and inspiration, as well as the following publications where poems in this collection first appeared:

Connecticut River Review: "Fire Dog"

Hoof Beats: "Questions I Never Asked My Father"

Nimrod International Journal of Prose & Poetry: "Skunk Cabbage"

Poets On: "A Simple Story"

Press: "Fox Run"

Reed Magazine: "The Slow Tide of The Dead"

San José Studies: "Red Rider, Red Rider"

The Spoon River Poetry Review: "Matthew"

Switched-On Gutenberg: "Glorios the Marigold!" "Under the Trees," "Donut"

The Texas Thoroughbred: "Claiming Race"

Yankee: "Swans on Christmas Night"

CONTENTS

THE MUSEUM OF NATURAL ART

In memory of my parents
Agnes and Red Pollard

and

for my children, Nicole and Matthew,
and for my brother, John Michael Pollard

Be kind, for everyone you meet is fighting a great battle.

—Philo of Alexandria

Survival is a kind of victory.

—Anon.

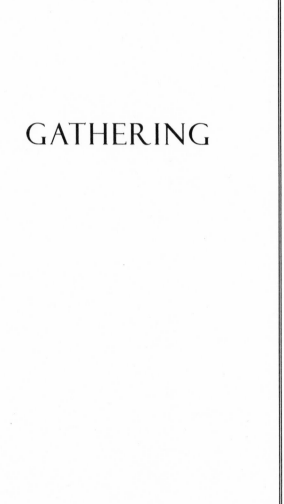

GATHERING

RED RIDER, RED RIDER

—for John "Red" Pollard, 1909 – 1981

I

You hardly were around, quick star,
dark storm racing lightning circuits of the track,

but when you came home, you came in gusts,
in gales of loud and louder,

until the banging of your heart,
your midnight valedictories from the roof

took up the moon's room in my night,
and days, you shouted down the sun.

II

When you'd leave, you'd leave enormous silence
in your wake.

The volume of your absence struck
the world deaf-still.

Even now that you are nine years gone,
I have to listen with extraordinary care

to hear the starting gate's bell gash air,
the thudding of those hooves less thundering than you.

GATHERING

He cracks the whip of his spine. Loosed
by rage, his small lick of flame body circuits
the room, an electrical fire,
fireball spinning in the dark.

   He is killing the tout.

Daddy is back from the track and drunk like
murder and I hide from him, crouching low
beside the piano with my fingers in my ears.

   Where is my baby brother hiding? Where under?

Daddy is howling so the wires in the piano hum high.
He howls, "Yardbiird!" to the ceiling,
his navy eyes roll, turn black.
He spins, he kicks the hassock,
wham! to the head of the son-of-a-bitch ponce
faggot lying horse pimp who led him wrong.

   Never cry, Jesus is nigh.

He is stomping the tout to death with
his boots—three running steps, a leap,
both feet on the wall at shoulder level,
stomp! He pivots, hits the ground, again
turns, runs, jumps on the wall.
His boots leave their heel mark.

   Jesus left his footprints in the sand.
   Yardybird will die.

Overhead, the lamp falters, brightens, falters.
He makes sheet lightning.
Mother and Auntie are darting in and out,
gathering the breakables in their arms.

Gather me, Momma.

Momma says over and over, "Sweet Jesus!" and
"Jesus, Mary and Joseph!" This is a prayer.
Aunt is muttering low bad things
about my father which she means him to hear,
which he hears, which craze him. He is
stomping on the dog bed.

Where are you, pup? Cougar dog? Cougie?
Where are you, Mi-Mi, my little brother?
Gather us.

Busybody Aunt crosses the room,
says in her hoity-toity voice,
"Oh, John, stop being such a fool,"
leans near as he spins by,
hisses, "You slubbering old sod!" She puts
these needles in his mind and he leaps
higher Wham! and "Bullshit!" and Stomp!
The mirror over the piano tilts, slides down the wall,
smashes. Glass flying, sequins in my hair,
diamonds on my arms. Pee scalds my legs,
my shame strong as fear.

"Mary, Mother of God!"
But where are you hiding, Mi-Mi Middilyhitten?

Aunt spies me, hauls me up. "Get up, now.
Stand on your two feet."

She pulls me to my room, her pearls
clink on the blue teapot in her other arm.
I crawl in bed fully clothed. Pee has
soaked to my socks, into my shoes, gone cold.
Aunt pulls the covers over it all.

Gather me, Sleep.

She leans down to me, her breath like the cellar.
She says words against Daddy in my ear.
She pretends to soothe me.
I do not hear her. All I hear is the stomping
and the tinkle of the glass lamp between
the shouts and howls and my mother weeping and
the plaster sifting down with the sound of ice.
All I know is the flash of lightning
under the door's crack,
the glitter of excitement in Aunt's small yolk eye.

Where are you, little Michael, little brother?
Cougar Dog?
Where do you go to, Daddy?
Night, gather us.

DRAGONSLAYER

It was blue and black and moved like a crack
across the baked orange earth.
It ripped towards the palmettos and
colicroot and its fat body
parted the tall grass like a Moses. Was gone.

Four, fubsy thighed, enthralled,
I run up the back steps calling "Snake! Snake!"
He opens the screen door. He scowls out.
He gets the spade from the shed.
I watch while he lopes to where I point,
the silver spade over his shoulder. He screams
"Aaaaaiguh!" and makes a demon face and
brings the snakesticker down and down and down,
grunting, "Uhhhh, Uhhhh, Uhhhh."
He stomps with his kangaroo boots,
his thin body leaping and stamping.
He snorts, he growls.

He finishes the thing.

He turns and says, "That hairbutted snake
won't bother you no more," and walks to
the pignut tree to sit under its dangling mosses
and smoke a cigarette.
My mother calls from the backdoor.
I go to her. "Did he kill the snake?"
"No, momma," I whisper, "the snake already was gone."
She laughs and covers her mouth.

I sit on the stoop and puzzle over this man
who is my father,
who wears cowboy boots,
who screams like a cougar,
who dances on invisible snakes.

BURNING

Eleven, brought home burning from the beach
so red it seemed my glistening skin could
split if tapped, so wretched in my pain
I sat in my room practicing death.
My mother, looking in, called
to my father, her mouth a twist
of pity and contempt, "Just look at this!
Burning like a brick in hell, silly twit!"

My silent red-haired father knew
about burning and went to get the salve
and smeared his hands and had me lie
on my stomach on the bed while he
worked me wordless, rubbed and stroked
to damp the fire down
and, burning from my bones on out,
flames hovering on my skin like St. Elmo's fire,
I clenched my jaw against his every touch.
My tears seeped in the sheet.
But neither would I speak.

My mother came again, stood at the door,
accusation like lye upon her lips.
"She's crying!" And my father stood,
looked down at me, at my face in the
pillow, my teeth gripping the pillow, my tears
in a sop around my head, and he gently
pulled the sheet up and tamped me down
the way you'd bury fire and left the room
and left the house and did not come back.

He did come back, though, in the morning,

smelling of hay and whiskey.
That whole day he hung around, not
touching, not speaking to me,
just being nearby.

HOW THINGS WERE

When he played his harmonica
he'd hunch over his lonely bony body
and blow "Old Black Joe" into the parlor
while Cougar the cocker spaniel, his head
thrown back like an operatic,
howled his agony or his ecstasy,
who could tell?

Sometimes he'd spring into a diggety dance
with Chinese leaps and alligator rolls,
the dishes rattled, the floor boards warped,
my mother fluttered, and the
dog lay low.
My brother and I, unstrung and
delirious, watched folded into
the drapes like spies.

Sometimes he'd stand over the piano
and pick out "Mother Dear, Oh Pray For Me"
with his two long index fingers, and when
he'd get to, "I wander in a fragile bark o'er
life's tempestuous seas," he'd pause,
then go softly to his old green striped
cigarette-holed chair and slide between its arms
to sip his whisky neat while
tears crept down his cheek
which we pretended not to see.

And that was how things were with Daddy—
all mixed up and no one knowing ever
whether to laugh or cry or hide under the bed.

When he'd come home after long times away,
my mother unsmiling would meet him at the door
and musingly welcome him with
"Well, John, you made it," and kiss him—
in ecstasy or agony,
who could tell?

CLAIMING RACE

During a race at Belmont,
my father went down with his nerved-up, crazy ass
horse, struck the turf and was trampled by the jam
of ton-weight hooves he had been
so excellently, so leanly leading.

On the cold track's clods,
he was given Extreme Unction, pronounced dead,
yet lived.
Newsmen by his hospital bed asked him,
"How come that you're not dead?"
"The devil had no stall for me," he said,
leaving them pleased they had a joke to lighten
the serious days of those who make an exegesis
of the *Daily Racing Form.*

And it's probably something like that—
most of our lives don't fill any particular purpose,
but our deaths will fill some space
being readied for us, but not ready yet,
some field where bluegrass begins to leisurely fail.

QUESTIONS I NEVER ASKED MY FATHER

Whatever possessed you to climb that first horse,
   clutch his barrel with your skinny legs
   and, hanging on to mane like mad,
   steal that crazy ride across the carnival field
   when you were ten and new to horses that same day?
What were you conspiring with them later
   when you stole into their stalls,
   the dark horses immense, breathing
   and stomping in the dark,
   rubbing their muzzles on your shoulder,
   their wet breath crismal on your neck?
Did you think you would marry them?
Did you think you would mount their
   roan backs and ride out your life in circles
   under Santa Anita's big blue sky?
Did you make up your mind to become horse?

And years later during those golden races,
   when you'd break from the gate
   did you think of anything but the blood rhythm
   of those hooves under colors,
   the furious speed you governed with your hands?
Did you urge on your bay in tongues?
Down the homestretch, were you filled with sudden
   love for the rider you were overtaking?
And later, in the shed-rows, with the grooms walking
   the hots, rubbing them down,
   in all that sweet smell of manure and hay and sweat,
   what did they say to you, the horses?
What did the horses say?

Tell me about the horses.

MAN WITH HAWK,
EDMONTON, ALBERTA, 1922

*—for John Aloysuis Pollard, 1875-1958
and John Michael Pollard, 1909-1981*

I brought the picture back
from Canada so my brother could see
how enormous the hawk was
our grandfather shot and posed with,
his arms outstretched,
the hawk's big head
not hanging over limp,
but upright, as if alive, his eyes
staring into the camera's eye
and his beak open as if to speak.
The hawk's long legs are heavy,
thick with feathers, as if he were
wearing a Chinese child's quilted pants.
His talons, in their rigor, are spread.

Behind the hawk, my grandfather,
a crack shot in a felt hat
which throws a shadow over his face
to the nose. Under the nose,
in black and white, is my father's
large mouth, half smiling, or
half not-smiling,
and behind the melancholy smile,
the wild and high Alberta sky.

On my desk now, hawk and man—
when I glance up and see them,

I like to squint one eye
and hold my thumb in air
to cover the body of the hawk
so the hunter has great wings.

FOX RUN

First time at camp,
first time away from home,
you stood before your cabin,
"Moose's Rock," and formally,
your eyes resisting a focus,
welling up, your voice
thin and trembly as the
high note on a flute,
you told me it might be time
for me to go (although
it was not time).
After the kiss, I pressed
money in your hand and
drove up the long dirt hill
away from you,
watching with grieving eyes
Shadow Lake to my right
sparkling silver-black through
the pines, wondering how
you'd do with your sunburn
and your bedwetting (knowing
you would stay awake all night
so you would not), when
something gold flashed
in the thicket and again,
again, like a gold thread
weaving through the summer
afternoon's dark leaves,
like a torch, lightening
and darkening and lightening,
like a bright bird,

like goldenrod, like the
yellow leaves of willows,
like a boy's golden head,
like you, it was you
running through the sumac
and the scrub pine,
running twenty miles an hour
up the hill beside me,
only far away,
until you disappeared in
laurel and my tears.

And you made out o.k.
and learned to swim and
learned to rinse your
sheets in the lake early
so they would dry, and
brought home a pinch pot
you had made and a certain
way of walking, a kind of
strut.
And though you're grown
and gone now,
I just want to say
that today, as I drove
Route 7 to Ridgefield,
I saw alongside of me
a red-gold fox running,
glinting in and out of sorrel
and high grass, blazing
like a brush fire getting up,
and I was reminded how
long ago you ran like the fox
and how you'll always be

the gold running through
my life, our lives separate
but travelling parallel
in love and time.

MATTHEW

My son, growing into manhood, not yet eighteen,
whose body I have not seen naked
since he turned twelve and private,
walks sure about the house,
carries his strength light as rope,
picks up a wrench, a pen, his guitar
with articulate hands.
His back is strong and broad, freckled.
Mornings when he walks solid to the shower
in a blue towel, I can see where his spine curves
down to the fine tuft at the cleft,
his legs covered with a fine gold illumination
of hair, the whorl of floss gold
spinning around his navel,
the small round garnets of his nipples,
his fine, long neck,
his head Etruscan, perfect.
And I cannot help the pleasure,
but take in his perfect body like my breath.

He comes by his strength through sleep,
which he goes into deep and stays long,
so late summer mornings I holler
to him to Wake up! Wake *up*! until
the day he slept till nearly noon and I
went to his room, angry at his sloth,
and ripped the sheet from him
(still sleeping) and looked upon
the dreaming limbs, the whole long length of him,
the curve of his back, the small hard buttocks,
the sweet snail of his sex

waking, wavering,
while he slept on,
lids quivering, mouth working on a word,
the breath coming so even, the heart beating so even,
the freckled hands, blue root veins at the wrist,
the long fingers curled,
the feet so long and white, so sure to run again.

He lay graceful, sleeping
in a pool of near-noon sun
while tears rose in me for his great beauty,
his sure mortality.

YOUR FATHER'S LEAVING

Sunday morning, cold morning,
your father is about to leave,
hunched in a corner with the shadows
waiting for the sun to rise
when he will say goodbye to you
as I had asked,
so you would know he was not spirited away,
there was a leaving here.

At 5:00 he claims you from your dream,
stands you up all frowsy for the news.
On his knees to be your level, he weeps.
He weeps. He cannot stop.
You look past him to the long stairway
and hold a curious smile.

"Please," I say, "please," until he releases you.
You step away neat, ignore us both
and in the morning chill
choose from your closet your best red dress,
your maryjanes,
put these on to go and tell the neighbors.
The street is empty. You kick some grass,
Then, caught by an idea,
you spin in circles down the hollow Sunday street,
your skirt leaping out from you like licks of flame.

COME AGAIN,
MY DAUGHTER

We have put the nails in place
and hammered shut our hearts.

You run a ring of fire around you,
stand at its center
burning with contempt.

I've summoned the coldest, darkest
river to island me.
I call and call,
"Come over! Come across!"
then greet you with
fear and ice.

There is no end to
our small cruelties.
I hear you give the killing sigh
of boredom to my words.
I mock your interests
with a belying grin.

We've wept and, with satisfaction,
watched the other weep.
When will it end? I think
this must be love, else
it would not cut so deep.

Our jealousies are fed by the
favors each is graced with.
You grow more lovely

as you grow away.

You stood the other evening
on the stairs, the porch light
falling on your fair face and hair
and on your mouth, so strong and stern
that love gave out,
my courage failed and I hung back
and did not kiss you.
Too late I noticed how your feet
turned in a little, like a child's,
the slight dejection in the way
you held your chin.
Just then you said, "I'll call you,"
with such a business voice
I waved, as to a stranger.
Said, "Come again." Whispered,
"Come again, my daughter,
Come again."

MICHAEL

All the small black ghosts of all the landfill crows
   you've ever shot,
all your good intentions and all your bad,
all your lost children dumped in pleasure's seed in
all the semis' sleepers and motels from New Jersey to
   San Antoine,

all the gypsy semis and their grand carnival-lit cabs,
all the big rigs hauling bananas, fish, steel,
all the gray wave wharves, the diesel fogged terminals,
all the long black lonesome highways of the night,

all the friends you've had who never let you down,
all those friends who never let you up,
all the truck stops' gritty coffee & country western woe,
all those juke box songs about the wife and son you lost,

all the paper horror books you read that help you
   understand desire,
all the gluey t.v. dinners in their bent tin foils,
all the scraggy strays you take in and name and love,
all the DuMonts, Snakes, Lillybeets & Rudys,

all the small-town diners' 3-buck meatloaf specials,
all the Little Feat and Ricki Lee Jones vinyls,
all the stained mugs of green tea to ward off cancer,
all your Basic cigarettes, all the blue, blue smoke,

all the paling blue in your bewildered eyes, the blue
   pallor of your face,
all the days and days and days of getting by,
all the long strange days,

all the nights just barely getting by,

all the dope and booze you've loved and quit and loved
    again,
all the bottles, needles, spoons, bags and vials,
all the morning after I-know-what-I-have-to-do's,
all the bone-crusher withdrawals, the methadone self-hate
    blues,

all the clinics, soup kitchens, flop houses, rehabs, small
    town jails,
all the dumpster-diving for the not-quite empties,
all the picking through the trash for what will yield some
    change,
all the fights you've lost defending a whore's hard honor,

all your Keep It Simples, your One Day At A Times,
all the roads leading back to Attleboro and Pawtucket,
all the crops of pot you farmed by moon in Seekonk fields,
all the sinkers you'd dive the Bay for to sell 10¢ for the lb.,

all the V.A. X-rays, all their probings of your gut,
all the days you've kept your strange integrity,
all your bafflements and dismays, your consuming list of
    wrongs,
all your hit-the-jackpot dreams, your lost entitlement,

all your ghostly paranoias, the bitterness of chances lost,
all the ebbing memories of your many gone or dead,
all your read-to-cloth "Fighting Knives," "Blade"
    magazines,
all the magnificent knives you made your art,

all the hours pressing steel to dad's old grinding wheel,

all the gorgeous handles of rosewood, amber, cocobolo,
  stag,
all the Bowies, dirks, boot knives, push daggers, skinners,
all the fine blades, polished, blued and tempered with
  your love,

all your tall and narrow body,
all your dancing, dodging kind of walk,
all your 2-pocket denim shirts, your army-issue boots,
all the silver Navaho belt buckles with the bear foot's
  claw,

all your long and delicate fingers,
all your rare, rare laughter,
all your life, my brother,
all your heart-breaking life.

TEN MILE RIVER

He was dying. We took him to the river,
the old river he grew up beside and loved,
and by its weedy banks he climbed up on
the big rust and moss mottled culvert, the water
glugging out beneath him, and he balanced there
above the river, unsteadily, slowly raising wide his arms.

We took pictures. Last pictures. Brother and
sister near the falls. Brother and friend,
laughing. Brother alone. Brother alone.

All afternoon the river moved slowly on toward
the falls, a painted turtle sat very still on a log,
sewing-needles and no-see-ums hung or drifted
in the heavy summer air, and the white clouds lay
across the sky like big indolent women.

The photos came back today.
My heart breaks, for practice...
in every picture we are black as cut-out silhouettes,
shades in the shadows of paper birch,
swamp maple and willow.

Behind us the river rolls a bright and shining blue,
and trees bind the horizon in greens and violets,
and the clouds...
the clouds are luminous as skin.

NARRAGANSETT DARK

—for my father

They led the horses away.
They tore down the fences.
The wreaking ball brought down
the grandstand, the clubhouse.
They plowed under the track kitchen,
the tack shop, the bettors' windows.
They burned the green barns.

When there was nothing of Narragansett
but a great empty space, the moon
glittered over it like a Vegas sign
and the wind blew dust across
900 acres to the Newport-Armistice roads.
The next day they paved.

Black asphalt covered the scent
of hay and the horse.
They built a drugstore,
a store for linoleum, and they
threw up subdivisions, aqua and mustard
and pink, whose mailboxes rusted
before they were sold.
Then they built a nursing home

where now the old jockey lay in a narrow bed.
He did not know where he was
so the irony was lost to him,
but he knew his wife would come
and wash him and light him a cigarette

and put the swatches of cotton
between his toes and pour him
a small cup of blackberry brandy.
Long nights alone, after the t.v. was
shut off and the brandy gone,
he'd listen for something.
All the long dark nights, listening.

One night a lean March wind
rattled the gate and his heart labored
in his breast and he rose up
for he heard what he heard—
their soft nickering and blowing, the thin
rustle of silks, the creak
of saddle and the tick
of hoof on stone.

And he left the bed and went out
to where they stood in the grasses.
He stood before them and
their breath fell on him like cloud
and he saw their great eyes pool the moon.
And the one waiting for him,
the one with an empty saddle,
was a bay.

He mounted up and they rode under the moon
and the wind flared the mane of his horse
and was hard and clean on his face.
The others galloped on either side, silently,
as if they were running on moss or flowers,
and he went with them where they took him
into the fields of night.

LAST LIGHT

If, some summer evening,
you were to come upon
my father's bones
under the ferns
by the dark and languid
Ten Mile River,
you would find them small,
for a man,
and note that the skull
was beautifully shaped.

You would note, too,
the unusually long and
narrow bones of his hands
bound together by the black rosary,
the fine shreds of green silk tie
still caught around the white
spools of his neck, and
the hair, translucent when
they buried him, now
perfectly clear, luminous as
spider's silk.

Many of his bones would show
old cracks and fractures—
his nose, ribs, one arm, a hand,
the hips, that terrible leg, the clavicle—
a chronicle of bad breaks
in a life of riding horses.

And then, if you were to kneel

and hold back the laurel and blackthorn
shading what had been his face,
you would find,
pooled in its socket like
a tiny lake among snow hills,
his glass eye,
steadfastly shining,
eternally innocent of the wild, harsh,
and gorgeous world it had gazed upon,
forever blue.

SALT

I don't care about spirit and
where the spirit goes after the body
quits and turns cold and solid
and there's no comfort there anymore.

I don't care about angels and
how they make their way to heaven
and look down on us from two trillion miles.
That's too far. That is never again.
That is gone.

I want my mother back.
I want her pale blue eyes to look at me
appraisingly. I want once more to hear
her say, "Kid, that's quite a rig."

I want to see her in the evening in
her mauve chenille, smoking her Tareytons,
reading her book by the light of the lamp
whose base is a brass chicken foot.

I want to sit with the blue willow teapot between us
and see her giggle into her napkin like a girl
over a silliness of my father's.

I want to see her scorn again,
the curl of her lip, her voice like an adze
when he'd come home late in a certain state.
I want to see her weeping by the window
while my brother, five years old, reels in the yard

drunk as a skunk on cough medicine. I want to hear

that mother's prayer to St. Monica again.

I want to see her faintly uneven top left lip,
her over-large earlobes, her exquisite nose.

I want to see her as we drive to the doctor
that last time, passing by the thrift shop
with the blue polka dot dress in the window.
I want to hear her say,
"Look at that! Silk, it looks like."
And then, with that hedged smile,
"Well! I guess I'm not dead yet."

Fuck spirits. Fuck death.
I want to buy her that polka dot dress
and I want her here to fill it with
those breasts and their rose-brown
nipples, her fundamental hips, her
elegant shoulders, those long white thighs.

I want the dress to billow with
her light, her heat,
so those dots move like constellations
around her palpable heavenly body
here,
            now,
                    in this manifest world.

FINIAL

Their lovely bones
beneath the snow
we stand on,
the setting sun
staining the birches gold—
we look to other graves
where red votive lamps
cast a hesitating light
and plastic poinsettias
splash bright as blood
against the snow.

We've brought nothing,
just ourselves to their
plain stone. Amid the graves
with flags, baskets of greens,
the gaudy plastic Santas,
angels, elves,
our parents lie alone
simple as plainsong.

And alone is our surname
on the granite—no dates,
no *Gone but not forgotten*,
no dogs, artist palettes, hearts,
no boats chiseled in the stone.
And we,
their son and daughter, their
yield, shield of their memory,
stand over them, stand for them,

until in the marbled waning light,

I gather up hard snow and
make a crumbly ball and place it
on the top curve of their stone
where its ice shines green-white,
spare as a moon.

ROUNDS

On a long and winding train ride
through southern country,
someplace you've never been before,
you might pass a certain place where, say,
three pines grow alone in a yellow field,
and an old grey horse stands still as stone
beside a tattered billboard. A crow flaps off
fretting the grey edges of memory.
You know this place.

And one day you'll travel to Hartford, say,
or Shreveport. Perhaps there
you'll visit some old inn or school
where you'll find yourself in an oak walled room—
lancet windows draperied, a heavy picture of
two women over the fireplace,
the rich bookcased wall, the green glass lamp.
You'll remember the tear in the old leather chair.
There will be a dreamy stir of dust motes
and you'll sense the silent others in the shadows,
attending.

Walking one fall late afternoon to Dalton's Pond,
the maples shifting heavy shadows over the road,
you realize someone is with you,
you can smell her perfume.
You stop very still. You listen. You breathe in her
fragrance, and very quietly, without turning,
you beg her,
   Tell me who I am.

SCARS

INTRODUCTION
TO THE SPIRITUAL LIFE

St. Leo's basement,
down there in the serious dark,
bumping, fumbling,
the air raid siren wailing,
we knelt bent over,
our hands on our heads,
crouched in the dust like
so many turnips waiting to be
harvested. The nuns
in their black robes
swished up and down the rows,
our own scarecrows,
rosaries rattling like bones,
black straps slapping,
hissing "Silence!" at the
small nervous giggle.

And down there in that heavy dark,
each Lent we witnessed
(for a dime) sweet-faced Jesus
murdered on the tattered screen.
The projector would break down
somewhere near Gethsemane,
exposing our stunned dread,
snapping us to reality.
But reality was up there on the screen
and when those spikes tore flesh,
the bitter sponge sent up
to that poor downturned mouth,
sorrow dense as drowning

filled our lungs;
we were sodden with it for days,
remembering the agonized eye,
the cry for "Father! Father!"
going unanswered, as usual.

Down there in the basement
where we were sent when we had disobeyed,
blinded and buried, both,
we could only hear, far and faint,
the trucks rumbling in the street,
the bell of the changing class,
the scraping overhead
of a hundred wooden chairs.
We shivered in the darkness
waiting for the hoof-footed devil
and his slavering rats
until, over time,
that dark became a place
to suffer freely in,
to luxuriate in alienation,
to watch the dust motes drift,
to feel the rapture of
the placelessness of blackness,
to imagine,
with all the power of darkness,
new, brave sins.

DONUT

—for Elaine Bloomer, wherever you are.

Fat, organdy-ruffled, curled
and mean, Elaine would lean
across the couch and in silence,
without expression, like
a scientist probing a worm,
she'd pinch the skin
on my skinny arm
between her fingernails
until a bright pearl of blood
appeared, red as

the jelly spot at the end
of the donuts her starch-aproned mother,
grandmother and aunt—all bounteously fat—
would bring on doilies of white paper and
a silver dish. Oh, the richness!
Oh, the smell of dough and sugar
in that mad and manless house! The reek
of butter, batter and sweet, sweet cream!
Vanilla's fume, scalded milk and ginger,
snuff of nutmeg, caramel and smaze of lemon rind!
Oh, oil of grenadine!

In my mother's prudent kitchen
dessert was Sundays only.
Friday, codfish. Back Bay
baked beans and brown bread Saturdays,
and through the week, leeks, ham stock and

cabbage oppressed the air.
Organdy was for the altar,
doilies were a Protestant excess,
and men and dogs were everywhere.

But, for that dusted donut, that fatty sac
of quivering cherry gel,
that powdered, pregnant blim of ruby sweet,
I'd spill my blood each week and never sing,
and sit with fat Elaine upon the couch
to eat the goddamn thing.

WILD THING

I have long admired the heron
that stands for long hours in still water
not thinking of his career or the news,
but standing because he is a heron
and knows who he is and what a heron does.

And the great tiger that ate twelve people in Karachi
felt no guilt and licked the platter clean
because he was a tiger busy doing tiger things,
and nothing else needed to be explained.

The animals, they don't gripe about their in-laws
or deal with shrinks or engage in kinky sex
or change their spots or colors or their spouses,
they just do and do the thing they do the best.

My first time, in Eddie Gemza's pool with Eddie,
out under the stars and liquid as a fish,
we played until he slipped it in without a warning,
so I bit his finger to the bone—he lost the tip.

And it was wild to see the blood torpedo the chlorine
and hear his swears and screams beneath the moon,
and it was wild to feel so wild and satisfied,
to taste of blood and know just who I am.

KISS

I was the high schooler awkward and shy
coming from church
on an August morning
in the two-toned DeSoto with the
clank in the rear.
He was the gas pump boy
at the Texaco station who said
he needed to hear the clank
in action.

We are the kids who drive
the hot and dusty country roads
of Seekonk,
windows down, wind flicking
my hat's flocked veil, his arm
out the window holding up the roof.

Past corn stands, watermelon stands,
cows, crows, and barnsmell,
past miles of shade trees,
past old tin trailers rusting in the weeds,
to a small dirt clearing in the sun,
where rock ledge and pines surround us
like an amphitheater.
Here
he stops the car and turns
and, barely smiling,
takes off my little rosette hat
with the veil, my white crocheted gloves,
and lays them carefully on the dashboard.
I am not afraid.

His lips, burnt by the sun,
his hands, the nails oil-edged,
touch me everywhere.
The sun blazes. The yellow dress
with the Peter Pan collar falls away.
Wordlessly we cling and kiss,
sweat and touch. His body
smells of sweat and socks and gasoline.
Bits of tobacco from the cigarette
crushed in his shirt pocket
stick to my shoulders,
fleck my small bare breasts.

He shrugs from the shirt
with the Texaco star,
eels from his oily trousers.
His sweating body glistens
like a molted thing, and
there's a port wine stain
like a Maybelline kiss
high on his thigh near his cullions.

Bees. Sun.
The black and pungent pines.
Yellow haze burning off yellow fields.
When he covers me,
his love cry throws crows in the air.
I bloom in his arms like mimosa.

FOUNTAINS

The giant
lying on his back in the park
is a statue.
One leg is bent at the knee,
the great calf of the other is
balanced on that knee
perpendicularly,
the huge toes curled in pleasure.
His arms are raised straight up, his fingers
stretched wide as though startled
by joy or holding some invisible delight.
The bottom of one foot, a wrist,
his massive thighs and chest,
are weeded with a stemmed and curly fern.
His giant head's thrown back, his eyes
bald and blank as ecstasy.
The lusty mouth is puckered in a kiss
and from between those lips he spews
a clear gush of water up
three feet or so before it turns to
splash back down upon his face or
chest or you—depending on
which way, how hard, the wind is running.
His genitals are hid in the crossing
of his thighs, but those with eyes
will know their size and can surmise
what pleasure in them lies.
His bronze body's brown, like earth.
All around him the hibiscus and the
marigold glow red and gold
while all above him clouds roll on,

roll on all day,
and nights, the moon and stars shatter
in his pool and recollect to shatter
and recollect.

I love to watch the giant and his water.
I see myself naked and amused astride
his loins, riding him,
my arms upheld like his
to catch the day,
or my legs wrapped around his
shining chest and catching
all the water he throws into my
own wide-open mouth.
On hot days, I will sit upon his eyes,
his great nose between my thighs and lean
to net his water on my nipples,
my two breasts divide the waters in
two halves of sympathetic ripples so
I become a fountain, too, and
feed the green-gold pool.

The giant lies and interviews the skies
and spits, with droll insouciance,
in heaven's eye.

HIS ANSWER

The tall girl in the supermarket wears
blue jeans tight to her skin as wet Kleenex,
walks with an arch to her back that lifts her
melon breasts high, like an offering.
Her red blouse stops just under her breasts,
hangs out from her body
like the tablecloth for a feast.

She's just dismissed the tangle-haired
boy she's with, calling him an asshole
at the checkout counter,
has gone looking for the refried beans
he forgot.
She's tossing her long black hair,
her golden earrings swing and flash,
her high heels tap like a whipping stick.

Now everyone who was looking at her is looking at him,
expecting to see a man who is embarrassed or angry.
But he's just watching her with a dusky look
of patience and certitude,
the way the lion tamer holds a
spirited cat in his vision,
croons those soothing, sleepy words,
anticipates the keen satisfaction of the taming.

A SIMPLE STORY

When the man makes love to his wife,
he thinks of his student on the window aisle,
imagines her long blond legs wrapped
around him, her yellow hair falling like silk
around their kiss and, under his urgent hand,
his wife's plump breast becomes
the student's wrapped mallow rose.
He rises to the length of her.

When her husband is making love to her,
the wife summons up the boy who rakes
their leaves and who, that evening, she saw walking
with his dog up the hill to meet the moon.
She remembers topaz eyes, imagines his great
need of her. It is his lean and shuddering flanks
she rears to meet.

Across the dark town, the student is looking out
the window and dreaming. She is looking
at the moon and twisting her yellow silk hair.
She examines her long bare feet and finds them
unexpectedly beautiful. She feels sudden changes
in her body. Her cells speed and swell.
She walks her room, she looks at the moon,
She cannot sleep.

The boy sits on the hill with his dog
enduring swift insistences in his body
which cause him to rise and run
back and forth over the hill's crest,
the moon to his left, the moon to his right,

his dog panting at his heels. Later, he walks home,
spent. He makes a large sandwich, eats it in his room.
He cannot sleep.

The next day the student and the boy meet on the street—
a simple story: the girl pets the boy's dog.
The boy laughs about something. The dog wags his tail.
It's all as if they've met somewhere before.

The man learns through her school friends
of his student's new love. She dreams out the window now
and does not hear his words, his words, his words.
And the wife never again sees the boy walking alone
with his dog at night.
The blank moon rides a barren hill.
Now, when the man and wife make love,
it is gentle and compassionate
and sad.

LATE AFTERNOON, THE BIRDS, LEAVING

On your book-strewn table
I clear a small space and place there
the beer you've offered in a wine glass.
I twirl and twirl the stem
with a prayer-bead user's rhythm.
The last of the day's sun strikes the beer bubbles;
whole small worlds explode.

You are telling me—it is some news—this association
I'd thought was love
is no good. This you absolutely know, you say,
the way a body knows why it rejects an organ.
(How the mind admires the smoothness of a metaphor
even as the knife drags ragged through the heart!)

Sitting across the room, so erect,
an arm on each arm of your chair,
you look so much like that statue of Lincoln
there is no doubt that you are being just. But I
am feeling anyhow the most grave pain,
and wiring together—
the way they wire old broken gravestones—
my face, to keep face,
I listen carefully. I meet your eyes.

But at some particularly exquisite point of pain,
I look outside the window
for a reminder of life beyond this room.
And over the roofs,
far down the road on a telephone pole,

a blackbird is sitting very still.

And what I am thinking is:
    If I can keep together until you are through and done,
    keep from showing centuries in my face....

And what I am also thinking is:
    It's funny the way a bird will almost always choose
    the highest place around on which to sit—
    the peak of pine, the steeple,
    the masthead's tip....

Then I picture all the high world's birds'
honest needle beaks hungering for heaven,
with their plain staunchness, their frankness of desire,
their simple loyalty to hope,

and rise and take my leave of you in silence,
almost gracefully,
as a bird blown by terrible winds
can make the free-fall from a great height
seem intended.

NOVEMBER

The deer hangs head down
from the big oak in the yard.
She is cut down the middle
and emptied. Her eyes are open,
her legs straight out,
heart-shaped ebony hoofs
inches from the ground.
She swings a little in the stiff cold wind,
her white tutu tail turning dreamily.
She could be a wind-up deer in a
Christmas window, pirouetting
in black glass shoes,
her outrageous incision just
a long red ribbon, shining.

Around her in the yard,
summer's cartoon plastic toys—
a red slide, a yellow dandle,
two blue broken pails.
On the deck above them
squats the black gas grill.

Two men who had been hosing out
the deer are now measuring and hammering up
a remote-controlled garage door.
A radio is playing, "Nobody Loves Me
Like You Do." The old white bulldog dozes
in the lawn chair while the leaves fall
around him. One house down,
a neighbor hangs out her clothes.

~   ~   ~

This is what Miguel left when he died
this morning—this plain, strange, ordinary life.
His breath has gone out into the yards.
We inhale him.
He's taken up residence in our cells.
He enters the white dog's dream.
He binds with the pale inner rings
of the oak. He slips away into the river.
He flows out.

Miguel has died. Nothing will change.
Local 101 without him will still build
the sets for jazzy Broadway shows.
His little red car will bank back roads
under someone else's verve.
The jetty he fished from on cool spring evenings
still drowns and surfaces with the tides.

And we still dance, though in a smaller circle.
And we still carry on our private industries.
Leaves will be raked, the deer eaten,
doors will open, doors will close.
But lashed around our rude and gutted hearts,
imagine red, red ribbons.

> —*for Miguel Rodriguez*
> *who died of AIDS*
> *on November 11, 1999*
> *at age 47*

LETTER TO A YOUNG POET

I hope you know what it is
to walk a long road
on a bitter cold night.
A road with no sidewalks.
Perhaps one or two garbage trees
shove their hysterical bones
through a chain link fence, or
a white plastic bag hanging from
a roadside sign collapses and
fills in the wind like a lung, or
a pair of sneakers jitters from
the telephone wires like
the feet of someone just hanged.
The halogen landscape is sick.

I hope, no matter how warmly you've dressed
or how short a time ago you've eaten,
that you'll let yourself down to
the distress of the dark, to the cold.
I hope you come to understand
as you hunch by the crooked apartments
with their many cozy lighted windows, or
the house where smoke
curls like comfort from the chimney,
that no one knows you, that
no one has ever known you.
I hope you will begin to know
what it is to be a night traveler,
sick, without, lost.
I hope you can despair.

I hope you do not try to cheer yourself up

by attempting to convince yourself
there's beauty in this ugliness, or
by thinking that
soon you will be home, or by being
optimistic, comparing yourself favorably
with a cripple or a fool.

I hope you allow yourself,
on your dark walk, to know how
alone you are, to go down to
the bottom of your loneliness,
to feel the truth of that so that,
when you do arrive at the place
you think of as your home—
a warm, well-lit and tidy place—
you will not recognize it as your home,
nor will the hat on the entryway mirror
or the photo of the man on the wall
seem familiar.
I hope you will never again feel
entirely sure of yourself.
This is what I hope for you—
that your eyes will see in the dark.

IN GRATEFUL RECOGNITION
~ OF ALL THOSE WHO ~
SERVED OUR COUNTRY
~ IN TIME OF WAR ~
THE TOWN OF STRATFORD
DEDICATES THIS MEMORIAL
A.D. • 1931

The statue in the park is breastless, but
a woman nonetheless. She sits erect,
broad browed, long robed, staring towards Main Street,
her throne high above the granite names of the elect
who unselectively were slain in war.
She holds a knife hilt (its bronze blade long gone),
and on the other arm, a massive eagle shield
erosion's pitted, pigeons roost upon.
She's laurel wreathed and heavy sandal footed,
her face serene beneath green streaks like grief.
There's a bronze dove beside her—and in her lap
what I'd always thought to be small scraps of leaf
or trash, up close are forty copper stars
graved into her thighs for every death, like scars.

THE MILLERS

All through the house
the miller moths float
so slowly you always miss them,
and when you do clap one,
fuse it to the wallpaper or curtain,
it leaves its shadowy imprint
like a Nagasaki victim's ashy negative on a wall.

The walls and ceilings of my house
are haunted by these small dull ghosts.
I always think, when I stalk the moth,
"This is the absolute last miller."
But it never is.
One rises up, swims slowly in some other room,
as the memory of a lover you could not win or kill
will drift forever though your mind.
Will not die.
Leaves a shadow.

WINTER'S COME

What I remember is your mouth,
firm and sweet as the flesh of the plum,
the way your tongue would idle
like a small sweet snake
among the stones of my teeth.
What I remember is lying naked with you
happy and languorous
all the summer afternoons by the lake's edge.
We'd watch the swans turn and turn.

There is a dying that comes slow.
The heart hangs on
the way the leaf hangs on the oak all winter,
refusing to let go, swinging in circles
to the measure of the wind.

Your lips! Do you remember how
you would kiss me on the lids,
first one, then the other?

LOVERS IN THEIR AMBITS,
ME IN MINE

The places where I like to walk
are also places where the lovers go.
I'll walk along the empty beach at dusk
while the sun's torching the horizon
and the island ferry is beetling
its little lit self
into the dark side of the world,
and as I'm climbing over the breakwater,
there they'll be,
dovetailed in each other's arms,
snug tight against the seawall's boulders
so I only notice them after I've
rattled shells into their spell.

Or sometimes I'll be walking down
the River Road making note of
three swans all twisting their necks
to the left in a loop so they are
their own feather boa,
or poking a big dead fish
lolling on his picked clean spine,
his head nodding yeses with the river flow,
when—Sweet stoats!—there the lovers are again,
sweet breathing in the rushes,
kissing wild.

I avoid cars. If they're parked
down near the dock when the tide is
turning the river around,
when the wind's licking up

the boozey waves like a drunk
and the moon's upstaging the sunset
so the moon's on one side of everything
thin and cool as love's pimp
and the red sun's on the other
like an old showgirl fan-dancing
herself off stage—
you can bet, on those evenings,
they'll be lovers inside the cars
fogging up the windows,
fiddling with lips and zippers,
hose and noses,
setting off the horn,
French kissing their way
to Morocco.

And I'll be looking the other way,
pleased, and in a funny way made shy,
picking lupine off the banks,
luffing alone across the meadow home.

LOVE POEM

Out of work, for cash I model
for the artists' guild,
sitting on a dais like a queen,
the lights heating my skin,
my silk kimono, gift of the man
I love, touching me all over
like his beautiful blue and gold fingers.

My focus point is a single black leaf in the trees
beyond the window where the maple and
the willow meet, their green and red
commingling. The clouds passing
darken and lighten and darken the leaves,
and when the sun breaks through suddenly and fiercely,
exultation so keen erupts in me, I know
the purpose of life is joy.

There is the soft intimate scratching
of pencil, charcoal and pastels on paper.
The artists, backlit, move shadow-like,
towards me, or away. One man makes small
gruntings in his throat while he paints,
like a man digging a grave,
or making love.
I do not see the artists' eyes, but I can feel
their eyes' intensity, can feel how
objectively and lovingly I am being seen.
I am being created. I am being laid down
on their paper.
They are making me theirs.

Slowly I move out of myself,

slowly I leave my flesh.
I no longer feel my body
and I can see, beyond the pane,
faces in the red and green and black leaves.
White eyes, red eyes glint and glow.
Leopard. The leaves shift. An Aztec boy
studies me. Shadows.
A black-eyed woman appears
shaking red lilies in her hair.
Once I startle to see my own face,
completely white and upside down
in the willow tree, my hair
pooling in the crotch of the trunk.
The wind harries the leaves.
I disappear.

When the hours are up
I am paid and, cash in hand,
standing dazed and muscle-trembly
in the blue kimono printed all over
with a thousand brilliant origami cranes,
I am feeling like a geisha
after hours of fine loving
who holds in her palm what will buy her bread,
having already drunk the plum wine.

SCARS

There's the one inside you cannot see—
the tonsils have been tonged and gone
(how humorous are tonsils!).
Imagine that scar to be red
and to have left me with less of a song.

A tiny mark holds at the corner of
my eye where once a cancer, that old crab,
clawed in. Now that lid's stitched narrower—
where half my face looks honest, trusting,
that eye being round and blue,
the other half looks cool and shrewd
and not so true.

Snips and sutures at my other mouth
where babies howled forth. Such
big babes! Large beautiful heads and
good strong shoulders.
Would there be scars for such a reason?
Maybe only thin pink lines, like
the signatures of bees.

There's my left ear, stitched back on after a
Van Gogh headfirst from a tippy chair
into a can of paint. Paint all over me,
the doctor nixed the color for the wall.
"Day-Glo Neo-Emu Blue!" he rued,
where it was irises I saw.

Hidden in my nest of pubic curls
is a pencil-fine line where they went in

like miners with their little light
and cauterized the tubes so no eggs drop.
It is a funny line, a fill-in-the-blank for a name
where no names will ever be.

Around my right nipple is a scar so fine,
so white it has a sheen like silver.
This mint nipple is a work of art. But though
my breast's stayed with me, all its feeling's gone.
No lingual lover can suckle sense
into its silver aureole.

There's the head: a dent on top, a small
hollowed place where, when I was a child,
a gold and radium-treated seed was dropped
to kill a tumor budding on my bonce.
Now nights on walks in my old neighborhood,
as I pass streetlights, they go out, come on.

Like the frost fern etched on a winter window, or
the faint memory of a palm's frond laid against
    hot skin
is the fine white splay of claws the cat set in
from my neck down to my shoulder to my chest.
He didn't want the bath and where a cat says No
to a human's idea of what is good for cat to alter,
blood is thicker than water.

My body's a passport stamped over
with the indicias of strange countries
I've survived.
But there are invisible scars, the sorrow-scars.
These lie hidden in the small ventricles
of the heart and never heal.
You cannot see them but they bleed

one drop of acid an hour
to keep me from going soft and too content.
These are scars that on a cold and truthful night will ache
and which, just to feel more fully live,
I finger for the pleasure of
the pain.

THE MUSEUM OF
NATURAL ART

SKUNK CABBAGE

"Skunk Cabbage sprouts so early in the spring
that the heat of cellular respiration resulting from
its rapid growth actually melts snow or ice round it."
   —*Audubon Guide to North American Wildflowers*

It was spring, or
supposed to be.
I went for a walk
in the woods.

It was colder than winter,
the cruel damp and the watery sun
were a discouragement to the soul
and the trees all grey and bare.

A little creek
at the bottom of the pasture
crept over stones and dead leaves.
The stones were rich colors

but when I chose one rose rock
and one a glittering grey
and another a bright orange
and dried them for my pocket

they went dull and ordinary.
Heavy boredom swathed my mind
like cobwebs. The earth was merely
grey matter.

I saw it then, poking from the marsh

like a little cobra's head,
the only live thing aside from
one brown non-singing bird.

The Turkish curl, the
sweet and stubborn spathe of
green and purple, the thick imp of,
the nerve, the élan

of the early skunk cabbage!
I knelt down
in the marsh, bringing my face
low to the ground like a praying Arab

and peered in to find
under the hood
the littlest white flowers clustered
on a knob—a bride in a chapel.

From the skunk cabbage, the
delicate smell of rotting garbage
oozed intimate and carnal, sending
a pleasure through me like coming.

The impossible stink, the flower bride—
bouquet of beauty and decay—
you, Life, you, trickster, shameless

wizard, old magician,
you pulled me out of
that black hat—again.

—for Judy

GLORIOS THE MARIGOLD!

Oh, God, I love the marigold!
That little bunched up constipated stink,
that goat's breath gold, that
orange butch topped mop, that
funny frazzle headed December daring rag, that
low down hosanna,
that red-gold stamp of temper in the noon, that
squabbled orange botch of boutonniere,
that bright bark of joy in the yellow morning,
that coin of courage in the frosted night,
that flower I vase to gaze at for three weeks
before it dies of staring back,
that I take by the broken neck and gently pinch
until, soft as mouse's ears, its petals fall upon
the sill, where all winter long its dried gold soul
beats out the color glad.

DRAGON MEAT

Pricking my fingers on its needle nails,
lifting its stiff green scales,

    dragging my teeth down the thin meat,
    relishing its odd, mild, mildewy flesh

        layer after layer until
        I come to its purple nave and

                eat that

    scraping off the yellow-green fur
    like a scalping

        exposing its innermost center,

I chew and suck
its secret place

    eating down

        to its hairy little heart
        the haughty

            artichoke.

STEALING LILIES

" Some things you have to steal to own;
some things you have to own to live."
                    —Christopher Lord Dalton

                    I

Beauty makes you want to own it.
The art thief, working sheerly on nerves,
his mind and body in a state
of great steadiness and
concentration, so alert as to be
pure energy,
works with his surgeon's tools
on the painting he is in love with and
which itself is energy, the colors
trembling and swirling and finally
giving over into the hands of the man
whose heart is suddenly calm,
suddenly complete.

The soft, shy, blue-haired lady
is over in love with color and
things that shine. She answers the suited
salesman in the expensive antique
store, "Just looking," with such
a smile he smiles himself, and
with a little bow walks off to let
her senses be at play.
She holds in her trembling hands
a champlevé box, a wonder of its kind.
The fine enamels gleam, the blues and greens

on fire, reds as red as the blood
on the fields of Agincourt.
Too beautiful to leave, too dear to buy,
this shining box she presses to
her heart in a panic of desire
as she walks out into the sun
bearing beauty, disbelieving sin,
for some commandment counsels her:
Beauty belongs to those who
love it best.

II

In my neighbor's field, strange purple lilies
grow unseen, puffing fat and waxy, about
to burst and splay their great mauve centers
wide as an innocent bride whom lust's surprised
and made to open herself. It's night.

There is no moon. I'm in the old man's field
feeling blindly along the fence's picket tips
for the rubber bands I've wrapped
to mark the places where the lilies grow.
I feel down the swollen lily stalk to

its base, mark off a hand span and
rock the spade into its groove until the
lily gives, its damp roots lift massed and
curled, rich as a plump woman's quim.
The night is drenched in honeysuckle

and the lovely scent of skunk.
Way down the road, a dog stands

tense as a guy wire under a yellow porch light.
He listens for the slightest scrape
of spade on rock or rasp of latch

on the field gate. He trembles to see.
So do I. Five lilies in the sack,
I keep close to the trees, creep home
to plant them this night near my old stone gate.
To own.

TO CONSIDER

Eighty degrees and a high wind—
who could believe such sumptuousness?
The peonies are so fat they lie down.
The forbidden purple of the Byzantine irises,
their frilled and membranous flesh,
is temptation and ruin.
The old pine leaning into the sky
is covered all over with a million new
tiny gold cones like little Chinese babies' pricks.
In the dark caves of the pine branches,
    the black crows scream in exultation.

When the world can be like this,
with the high swaying sycamore
and the poplar tossing in the wind,
and the crows and bluejays strutting about
in their simple lordliness,
and white elf flowers spy in the grass,
and the honest worm's under it all,
when the world can be like this,
    why do we let the moneyman break us?
When the sky pours down its blue balm
and the wind curves to our throat,
when the rain fingers our hair,
and the tolerant earth carries our feet,
    why do we let the coin shut our eyes?

FIRE DOG

I wish I could shake myself all over
the way the black lab will shake herself
coming up from the river with a stick.
She starts the shake before she's fully out.
The second her nose and flews are clear,
her head begins to whir, blurs, jowls fly, ears vanish,
then her shoulders emerge, dragging water,
and she begins to shake harder, even as
the hind of her still struggles to gain shore.

She shakes mightily to throw off the river's weight:
the head, the ribs, the hips, the legs, the tail
all in a tremendous ague shaking separately
in a different direction and manner
as if possessed by some holy fit
or performing a fiendish tarantella.

The crystal shower of river hurling off
blurs her outer form, magnifies her edge
so the drops she casts, hit by the light,
create a water aura
and for some moments in the sun
she is a crystal fire dog
shaking like a flame in a high wind.

THE SEAWEED KING IN THE MUSEUM OF NATURAL ART

There's always some marvel on the beach.
Last winter a crusty barnacled piano washed up
upright on the shore, ice on the kelp-fringed keys.

Now here's a sculpture—six feet tall and looking like
a man on horseback. Up close, nothing but the miraculous
singularities of its parts: a small yoked tree, denuded,

tubular things from which rotted orange buoys hang,
one yellow detergent bottle on a rope, a red paisley scarf,
a skyward pointing branch crowned by one blue rubber ball,

and fitted in the crevice of an upright driftwood shank,
the small toy figure of a fierce yellow-haired, red-eyed
man in a half squat, his muscles bulging like bread loafs,

(the tiger skin loincloth bulges too),
and all around his throne green seaweed drapes
from branch to pipe to tube like moldly lace.

Little white god, oddly wrathful, crouching in your grotto,
grimacing at the waves, thank the artist who built
your wilding temple, thank him for your royal seat of state,

and praise the setting sun. For when the moon
sends down her thin white light, the tide will bring
dark waters cresting over you and all your trappings,

and not your muscles nor your grimace, nor your
red and glaring eyes will stay the rolling waters,
nor keep the sand from ravaging your king's yellow hair.

FEBRUARY SUNDAY AFTERNOON

By the sea wall
a raw day and a razor wind.
The waves are rolled steel,
the sky a glaucous roil,
old snow lies rotted and leachy along the pier.
The feral cats hunch shivering on the wall
or slink dispiritedly among the rocks,
while the gulls sink their heads
under their wings, their
underfeathers blowing back.

No soul for a frozen mile around
but three old ones pressed close to one another
wrapped up tight as cigars—
the couple, their stooped backs to the seawall,
and the old man, grizzled, grinning,
green scarf whipping, facing them,
his whole face shining in a rapture
as he sings into the wind
in a frail pure tenor—

   ...and when the fields are fresh and green,
   I will take you to your home again.

Around the three the cruel wind circles,
hunting for entry into their fold.

WATCHING NIGHT COME IN

—Lordship, January 16

Down at the shore, a winter-weakened sun
gathers itself for a dying grasp at brilliance
with a sunset brief and bloody
as the last words of de Sade.

There are no waves, no sound of waves;
this silent sea is nothing I have known.
For half a mile out
the sea is slate crystalline slush
undulating under a glistening skin
back and forth, back and forth,
pulsing beneath its iced gray membrane
like something dark contained in something dark.
A faint sibilance comes through—sensed, not heard,
like the blood's rhythmic hiss in a mute's ear.

I climb the icy breakwater, edge my way out
to see in the darkening Sound
a moving going on in silence,
a heaving and a glittering,
a gathering of force.

In this sudden ending of the light,
something is beginning—
like the hard birth of worlds.

These will be dark ones.

THE SLOW TIDE OF THE DEAD

I

The tide leaves deaths like decorations on the shore—
wavering ribbons of empty blue and purple shells,
the arced bow of a dead gull's ribs,
the white crane flung against the jetty,
broken neck looped like an old bell pull.
A bluefish rotting in the sun
looks on vacant skies with small sandblasted eyes,
and all along the beach, the purple mussel shells
stick straight up, open in the sand
like tongueless mouths.

Once, after a winter storm, I found a drowned setter
the sea had put down as easily as if
he were stretched before a fire—
front legs crossed, the tail out straight and feathered,
and all around him, frozen to the sand,
the sea had laid died wreaths of green-black kelp.

II

From the thruway cutting straight through Bridgeport,
I have seen St. Michael's graveyard fill the field.
Old obelisks, huge-winged granite angels, crosses
have given way to common blocks of stone—
rows on measured rows of small white squares of rock
have moved, like ice floes, inexorably in.
The headstones have made headway in the wood,
taken over the trailer camp, the failing tool and die,

and the nine slum tenements on the Bridgeport line.
They have now come quietly to the highway's very edge
where life, all day and night, speeds ignorantly by.

THE NARROWS

Last evening I walked through the fog-eaten snow
to the place where the Sound narrows to the Housatonic,
and at the wharf, just at the dark outside of the
street lamp's circle of light where I almost walked on him,
lay a heron, a Great Blue, in perfect profile, perfectly dead.
I had that funny jump of the heart.
I stooped to see in the dark the long orange-rimmed beak,
the S-curved neck, one great wing fanned up,
his yellow-palmed feet.
A bit of streetlight caught his opalescent eye.

As I touched his frosted head, I thought of the suicide
from the Moses Wheeler Bridge two nights ago—a beautiful
(I say he was beautiful) 26-year-old "man"
they said in the paper,
but boy, really, after all, wearing no jacket, they said,
no ID, dark clothes, a scapular, no shoes. He left a watch
balanced on the railing.

The dark deepened. There was the letting go.
That zero moment when he stepped out into air like a natural,
where the wind laid a cold hand on his cheek
and billowed his outstretched sleeves, his hair streaming back
into fog, his whole body flowing through night's field
as the bridge lights, reflected in the water, rose to meet him
like the welcoming candles in a dark hall.

RIVER WATCHING

At the river,
autumn fog.
A small white sun trying
to burn through
and failing,
one lone fisherman on the dock
sinking his hopes into the
thick water.
The river, just turning tide,
unwinds for miles down its center
a ragged ribbon of tired froth.
Sailboats anchored on the
river's belly barely move.
All of them are white.
Across the wide river,
the trees are white. The gulls
dip and glide in silence.

I've come down to the river to
look at my life.
I let the river see me as I am,
my face slack as sleep, or death,
my eyes empty, old as the river.

The way the telephone line sags across
Shore Road, the way it stretches out
to nothing, disappears in fog,
instructs me in sorrow.

My life resists examination,
my mind meanders, twists and eddies,

evades the truth, snags on memories,
stagnates in the backwaters of fear.
I try to hold my course: look at myself.
What is it I am? What have I been?
There was some song, some dance,
despair, grief, romance, a life
as small as the little puff of
dust the road gives up under a
brief rain,
a scarcely noticeable life, not
particularly brave or good,
and the regrets are many.

The river knows me.
We are old friends.
Today I stand on the dock
in fog and fix the question:
And have I loved?
Slap & clug, slap & clug
against the pilings, the hiss of
current sucking on the quay.

A line of swans glides by, a white
adult on either end and seven cygnets
in between, large as the parents
but brown still, with lavender beaks.
They swim a straight and silent line
from Lordship town to Milford beach.
Now an oyster boat comes trawling,
little red light, little white light,
and there's the far green flash of the
beacon out in the sound.
Yes, I see the beauty in this world,

yet I could let life go and go on down.

Under the planks at my feet,
the river flutes beneath me. Adrift,
I am desireless at last.
When I was very young,
an old woman said to me,
"Survival is a kind of victory."
I forgave her because she was old.
Now I forgive myself for understanding her.

Up river, by the launching ramp,
where the gin pole looms up out of
the fog like a gallows,
there is a sign stands in the river,
"No Wake."
The river rides out silver into the sound.
Before it reaches the lighthouse,
it disappears into the silver sky.

COCK CROW

Before sunrise,
after the moon's gone down,
when the world is empty of light,

from the silence of black mountains
and the blacker valleys
comes the wild, unearthly keening
of the cock's crow.

It is answered by another cock
in another valley
and then another cock from a distant hill.
Like the dead in their perpetual lamentations,
they cry a round of woe
that rings the rim of the world.

Their keening enters into your dreams
in that no-time between dark
and first light
when you are gone out from yourself,
gone from your bed,

travelling the empty hills,
weeping, blind,
your feet cold upon the cold desert floor,
your hands feeling for the wind,

trying to get back to the dark place
you came from—
that pool of silence where
you lay desireless and empty,

made of nothing,
belonging to nothing,
drifting in the biding emptiness
before good and evil.

The cock crows.
The sun rolls up between
the mountains.
The dogs bark.
You wake to your familiar griefs.

UNDER THE TREES

I am talking about the heaviness,
the darkness of the trees,
of their green over green over green,
how they keep me under their emerald light,
as under water,
how they fold over one another in the night
like nuns in dark robes,
how they delete stars and cage the moon,
how they're always whispering or clicking
their leather tongues,
how they keep me from the horizon,
how they hem me in,
remind me I am small,
how they never let me forget myself,
how they keep the time, clocking the seasons,
filling me with urgency,
how they hold birds in their hair whose song is
my constant conscience,
how I can never feel the stillness because
their branches are swishing like a switch
holding me to my work,
how they are as beautiful and austere as
brides in their veils.
I am talking about how
the trees have spirits and they sing my name.
How I must answer.

LEANING IN

Lost for the last half hour
of a numbing winter's night,
driving the winding roads of Redding
alongside an endless lake which glints,
despite the darkness,
pale among the pines,

I pull off the narrow road
to read the map and am at once
enfolded by steep silence, thick black.
I turn the lights off, leave the car's warmth
and walk aways into the freezing wood.

The silence is almost absolute,
yet I seem to hear the lake's deep heart
pulsing the fine-iced water to the shore.
The black pines breathe and stir,
something heaves its wings,
the air is quick.

The lake rides up to the black sky
and the sky drops down and swims black with the lake,
and the lake and the sky and the pines
form a great dark round.

I stand on the edge
enduring a wild fear, a terrible expectancy.

PAEAN TO THE GREEN PARAKEET

Small green bodies
jitterbugging in the sun,
they screech like girls
discovered in a pool.
Green parakeets
in New England pines!
Neon oxymorons!

Always in the air, they jet
in spurts, falling and
rising through the air like
hurdle racers, zig-zagging
as if the air were mined,
and all the while
a parrot pandemonium.

I've seen them on the ground just once,
early winter at the wood's edge—
a green puddle of parrots.
Humpnosed, startle-eyed,
they pecked and mugged and
when they spooked,
they lifted into the air as one
green solid plate
to break against the
hard New England sky,
green pieces flying gorgeously
in twelve directions.

Birdnapped in Gualeguaychu,
shipped to New York,

a broken crate,
a fly-the-coop, and
this survival.
Wee escapees,
oh brave frivolities!
You endured that first cruel winter,
bringing your outrageous green and screak
to bear against the blue-gray sleet,
the skinning wind, the snow,
the dire black crow's
Caw! Caw!

A LITTLE ROCKIN', A LITTLE FOOLIN' AROUND

Three below and the river moves under ice
slow and blue as a vein.
The mallards swim in a numb huddle by the shore,
paddling, paddling to keep their piece of river free.
I feed them bread. They shout and bang heads.

I feed the gulls, too, holding the bread up high,
standing steady under an avalanche of wings.
So many white wings creaking and pounding
the air around me, I feel like some cracked saint
heaving into heaven.

The gulls hang over me, looking down
open-beaked, their eyes hard and
calculating.

A thunder like one-hundred bobsleds—
here comes Jake's old grey sheller
plowing up the tin river like a
can opener zipping the ice.
Great long cracks, like lateral lightning,
fork out before the pug-nosed prow.
Behind, the fractured squares of ice
quake and pitch in the wake.
How can he work the water for
oysters today, so cold?

Jake plows out towards the bay, but
turns at the mouth, comes back by
the far shore shooting his lightning,

rolling his ice. The world splits and warps.
He turns again, down river by the marina,
comes back around, tightening his circle.

I think old Jake's gone mad, trying to
kill himself, maybe. But this time
as he bumps by, carving up the river,
he swings his blue cap at me
and laughs. I wave and laugh, too,
and he goes on cutting the river's throat.

Maybe he's drunk. Maybe the cold's
got to him. Maybe he thinks he'll tame the river
the way I'm taming the gulls.

Or so I'm thinking when a herring gull
snares the whole bread bag. Off he wallops
towards the marsh, fifty gulls galloping behind
like a mob of spirit muggers.

Jake, Jake, beware!
You wouldn't last a minute under the river's
silvered tongue.
Jake is turning hard again, aiming for the
thirty-foot floe mid-river.
The flat-bottomed sheller yaws and humps.
He's got the radio turned up high, his
invitation floating out to the frozen world—
   Come on, baby, let's go downtown,
   do a little rockin', foolin' around.

The red and black and white shark's mouth
painted on the prow
eats river.

AKBAR, HERR CORMORANT,
MY SEA CROW

Out of a pile of sycamore leaves
an explosion of black and weed
and a crazed scuttling and dragging
and a black whirling like a panic
in a dark dream.

Then the sudden stillness.
Then an eye. Then a webby something.
The black takes form.
Against the yellow marsh grasses,
against the dying yellow light,
the black cormorant, all angles
and long stroke of neck,
as startling as a Chinese inkstroke on parchment.

I see no mark on him, yet
he reels, he pivots on his neck.
When one blue-black wing opens wide
pounding for a lift-off, the other folds in,
droops before his beak like a vampire's cape.
His grey webs cannot hold him to the ground,
he rolls, thrashes, spins,
and all the while his hooked beak opens
and shuts, opens and shuts in a terrible
mute scream.

Oh my cormorant, I've loved to see
you swim, your whole body riding
beneath the surface of the river,
your long black neck and head working

like a periscope, your head tilted back,
looking left, looking right.
That disappearing act of yours,
a split-second's soundless dive, then
the long wait and always you bob up
so much farther up or down river
than I had bet on.
Standing on a piling, your wings hung
out to dry, you look German, Herr
Commandant, Herr Cormorant, you
look Aztec, you look crucified, you look,
my cormorant, like a god disguised.

I name him Akbar and hood him
with my sweatshirt. Together
we head home in the dusk—a woman
somewhat leery of her crazy cargo,
such a large black bird, big as a goose!
A three-time struggler who manages
on the third to free his head and neck
until I give up
and carry him ahead of me like a black boot,
like the Ark of the Covenant,
like a radioactive loaf,
his long neck straight out
and peering into the gloom ahead, sleek
as an Egyptian.

At home I put him in a box, poke holes.
Tomorrow to the sanctuary.
I nick a feel of his black shining head—
soft as mouse's fur.
His hooked beak opens wide—inside all
pink and orange like a jungle flower.

I close him in my room away from
the trembling cat who is all wires and
cannot uncrouch himself.
I sleep.

The river rises under the moon
and a steady river-wind rides beneath the clouds.
It lifts the curtains and on its breast it carries
the silvery dink-dink-dink of the halyards
and the salt and the musk-damp of the river.
I wake once to the cormorant's thick fishy
smell, his quiet tappings,
his low guttural grunts in the dark.

I dream the long dive down in dark water
where shafts of moonlight silver the
slow sleepy fish. Above me the ceiling
of the river winks and sparks.
The eelgrass sways, the blue crab and
the green-gold lobster clack and creep.
Butterfish float by and the longfinned squid
and the glass shrimp.

The river moves all ways at once.

Wings sleeked to my sides,
black and swift as the river,
I run the river to my other life,
and the dark current carries me home.

SWANS ON CHRISTMAS NIGHT

The rare full Christmas moon
lay on the far bank of the river,
fat, elliptical, quivering,
like the bubble boiling out from
the glass blower's wand.
Along the coast, two green beacons
winked slowly in the windless cold
and the black river lay sleek and still.

They were just there—no dramatic
flying in on thudding wings
or gliding out of darkness into
the moon's white wash—
just there as I came down the hill
to the river. Eighteen of them
sleeping in the water,
heads pillowed on their own backs, or
holding motionless, looking
down into the water like long-necked
kohl-eyed, mooning girls
blooming white in the black night.

The swans rocked and slept,
the moon unmoored, drifted high,
grew smaller and brighter,
and a thin thread of cloud raveled across
the dark and mindful sky.

Photograph by Lynn Muniz

Norah Pollard was born in Pasadena, California, into race track life—her father was John "Red" Pollard, who became a national celebrity as Seabiscuit's jockey. After graduating from college, she lived and worked in England and Turkey. At various points in her life she has been a folk singer, waitress, nanny, teacher, solderer, and print shop calligrapher. Currently, she works at a steel company in Bridgeport, Connecticut. She received the Academy of American Poets Prize from the University of Bridgeport while studying under Dick Allen, and for several years was editor of *The Connecticut River Review*. Norah Pollard lives in Stratford, Connecticut.

COLOPHON

For their assistance in the preparation and promotion of this book, special thanks to Missie Rennie of CBS News, Pat Pothier of *The Providence Journal*, literary agent Robert McQuilkin, Jr., designer Sarah McQuilkin, archivist Helen Johnson, poet Gray Jacobik, and Laura Hillenbrand, author of *Seabiscuit: An American Legend*.

Leaning in is set in 11/14 point Times New Roman, with Felix Titling for titles and Goudy Old Style for embellishment. Graphic design by Ben Pollard and book-production by EPS Printers, Inc., South Windsor, CT.

For additional copies
of *Leaning In*
or other Antrim House
titles, visit your local
bookstore or contact
the publisher at:

Antrim House
P.O. Box 111
Tariffville, CT 06081
860.217.0023
eds@antrimhousebooks.com
www.antrimhousebooks.com